How to create and deliver great speeches

A seven day approach

Templates, checklists and tips to become a better public speaker

Table of Contents

Last saved: July 15, 15

Last saved: July 15, 15

Purpose

Why read this e-book?

- Leverage templates that you can pluck straight out of the e-book and use in your public speaking engagements.
- Have handy checklists that you can use to make sure that you have not missed anything in your speech.
- Need to do a speech and have no time? This e-book will have tips and templates to structure your speech so that you can minimize the time spent in creating your speech.

What will I get out of it?

- I'm hoping that out of the first read, you will pick up a few tips and templates here and there that you can leverage immediately for your next speaking assignment.
- As you progress, I am hoping that you will pick up even more tips and strategies. As the tips I share in this e-book are not complete list, I am willing to bet that you will pick up on things that I have not included (add notes or let me know and I can expand on it in another version of the book).
- Lastly, if you feel that you have mastered everything, the checklists and templates will help you expedite your next speech. There may be things that are not included in this e-book that you feel might work for you but you may not be sure about to include in your speech and to that I say: experiment! Try it out in a safe environment (like Toastmasters or with your close friends) before trying it formally and see how the audience reacts. It's important to understand how your audience will react to it, so you can know what kind of effect it will have on your speech.

Benefits

- You will have a greater understanding for exactly how you should be building a speech - you will never have to worry about what you need to do to craft and deliver a great speech as you only have to follow the plan that I have used for almost all of my 50+ speeches I have delivered in different situations.
- You will gain confidence in your speeches. Not only will you understand what specific things (body language, vocal variety, even the language you use) will affect the audience but you will use the right things to emphasize different parts of your speech to great effect.

- You will have the tactics and tips that I have used during my speeches, both when speeches are going well and when they are not. Learn from me so that you do not have to learn from your own mistakes.

- You will build a solid foundation for your communication skills which are paramount to all jobs, all relationships and in all areas of your life. Having great communication skills means better problem solving, better relationships, better leadership skills and much more.

The approach

Just before you start to write a speech (from scratch), I want to acknowledge the fact that this is not an easy feat. Writing and delivering a speech will not be a huge time commitment but then again, it also depends on why you are delivering a speech. For instance, a speech as a best man or maid of honour may not take as much time as a keynote speech at a conference (or perhaps require as much formal preparation). Although I will not be able to lay out all of the plans for every single speech you can possibly give, I believe you can adapt this schedule based on the length of the speech. For example, there is a rule of thumb that every minute of speaking takes an hour of preparation and based on that rule, and assuming that we all live busy lives and can only spend an hour a day to prepare and practice a speech, a 30 minute key note speech may take 30 days (which obviously can be longer or shorter depending on how many hours you practice each day). What I am proposing in this e-book is a 7 day approach to take you from zero to creating and delivering a solid 7 minute speech in a week.

My e-book will cover 7 days. The following will be covered on each day:

- Day 1 - Determining the purpose of your speech and initial outline
- Day 2 - Researching and developing the speech content
- Day 3 - Transitions and memorizing your speech
- Day 4 - Understanding and incorporating body language
- Day 5 - Understanding how to use your voice
- Day 6 - Full practice and crafting your introduction
- Day 7 - Final touches and delivering your speech

Day 1 – Determining the purpose of your speech and initial outline

Speech purpose

As a speaker, you have to understand why you are creating and delivering this speech. Do you need to make a presentation for work? Were you asked to do some in-person training for new employees? Are you giving a keynote speech at a conference? There is something in common with the answers to all of these questions: the speaker has a purpose that they wish to achieve.

Every speech has at least one general purpose and one specific purpose. Some speeches can have multiple purposes but the more specific the purpose of your speech, the more time and content you can devote to achieving that purpose. Sometimes, you may see a speaker go over their allotted time and this can be because the speaker has covered too much in their speech. It takes a special focus in order to really focus in on a specific purpose and to deliver a speech on that purpose rather than trying to cover everything.

Implicit in thinking about your purpose is thinking about the audience that you are delivering your speech to. What do they know about your subject? How easily affected will they be by your speech? Will they be convinced at the end of your speech by simple facts or will they need strong evidence/anecdotes to convince them?

If you have read my tips on making a speech more impactful, you will already know that every speech falls into one or more categories of general purposes:

- Entertain

A speech that entertains holds and captures the audience's attention in some way. I think many times, people might think that an entertaining speech is humorous but that is not always the case. A speech about going through puberty can be just as entertaining as a speech about your worst day ever. After the speech, the speaker's purpose (to entertain) will be achieved if the audience is captivated by the speech and generally feel in a better mood (smiling, laughing, etc.).

- Inform

A speech that informs teaches the audience about something that they might not have known previously. The speaker, in a way, is a subject matter expert and is explaining a concept, a theory, etc. After the speech, the speaker's purpose (to inform) will be achieved if the audience has a better understanding of the subject.

- Persuade

A speech that persuades tries to convince the audience about something (an opinion, a controversial statement, etc.). In a way, a lot of speeches fall into this category because a lot of speeches are trying to convince someone of something. There is also a subtle difference between a persuasive speech and a motivational speech: a persuasive speech often appeals to the logic of the audience whereas a motivational speech often appeals to the emotions of the audience. After the speech, the speaker's purpose (to persuade) will be achieved if the audience is convinced to change their views on the subject. If the audience may even consider changing their views; this could also be seen as a successful persuasive speech.

- Motivate

A speech that motivates tries to convince the audience to take action to improve (usually themselves). Again, you may feel that it is similar to the persuasive speech, but a motivational speech appeals to the emotions of the audience (though not always). Take donations as an example. Logically, we should all donate because we know donations will make the world a better place in some small part. Yet, I believe we do not donate because of the logical reasons, we donate because it affects us emotionally, whether it is because it makes us feel better or whether it is on behalf of a friend or family member. That is to say that you might be able to convince someone logically that something is the case, but you will not affect change unless you also appeal to their emotions. After the speech, the speaker's purpose (to motivate) will be achieved if the audience is convinced to take action (the speaker will define that action in their speech).

Once you start to understand the purpose of your speech, you can then start to understand what specific purpose your speech will achieve. The general purpose of your speech may be to motivate the audience, but what exactly do you want the audience to take action on?

Suppose I write a speech about the benefits of exercise – what are the general and specific purposes of my speech?

The speech can fall into many general purposes: the speech can inform the audience about exercise, the speech may persuade the audience about the benefits of exercise or the speech may try to motivate the audience to take action through small steps.

Once the speaker understands what general purpose they want to achieve with their speech, they may even refine the specific purpose so that it is better suited to the general purpose.

If I wanted to motivate the audience to take action through small steps, my specific purpose might become: convincing the audience to take a 15 minute walk every day.

Benefits of creating a speech outline

There are many benefits of creating a speech outline:

- It will form the foundation and delivery of your speech
- It will be easy to know what you are missing when you can see the speech as a whole
- It will help you determine the timing of your speech by how much content you have in specific parts of your speech
- It will help you rearrange the speech in ways to better achieve your purpose or deliver your message

Below you will find a template that I use to craft a simple, but effective speech. For the rest of the week, we will be filling in this template and I will be filling it out along the way to show you all the steps I take in crafting a great speech.

General purpose of my speech:	
Specific purpose of my speech:	
Speech title:	

Introduction	
Thesis statement	
First speaking point	
• Supporting fact #1	
• Supporting fact #2	
• Supporting fact #3	
Second speaking point	
• Supporting fact #1	
• Supporting fact #2	
• Supporting fact #3	
Third speaking point	

Last saved: July 15, 15

• Supporting fact #1	
• Supporting fact #2	
• Supporting fact #3	
Conclusion	

End of day 1 checklist

<u>Question</u>	<u>Action</u>
Do I know what my speech's general purpose(s) is / are?	Try to understand what state of mind you would like your audience to be in before and after your speech. This will often help in understanding the general and specific purposes of your speech. For example, do you want them to take action? Do you want them to be in a better mood? Do you want them to learn something new?
Do I know what my speech's specific purpose(s) is / are?	
Do I have an idea of what speaking points I will want to share in my speech?	Start to think about HOW you will achieve your speech's purpose. If you are trying to convince them of an opinion you have, what facts / evidence / anecdotes will support your opinion?
Do I have an idea of what structure my speech will follow?	Note that if you have been asked to give a speech, you may want to ask if there is a specific structure that they want you to follow. For example, for a speech that I did for Pecha Kucha, the speech format was 20 images, 20 seconds each image for a total of 6 minutes 40 seconds. Start to think about how your speech will move from topic to topic.

For this book, I will be creating a speech on getting the most out of your smartphone. I have also started to think about my three speaking points; however, these can be changed during Day 2 when I do some more research on the topic and understand how I will transition from one topic to another in a logical and efficient manner. I am also in the preliminary stages of determining how to structure my speech in a way that makes it easy to follow – for instance, right now I am thinking about a typical day in the life of a professional and what they might be doing in that day (eating, working, working out, sleeping, maybe shopping, etc.). If I can somehow organize my speech so that it matches those typical activities, it will help to give my speech a better structure and help the audience understand the speech better.

Note: I have not created a speech title, but it will be created as I start to flesh out the speech.

General purpose of my speech:	Inform, but also persuade the audience in a way
Specific purpose of my speech:	How specifically they will be getting value out of their smartphone (through apps)
Speech title:	

Introduction	
Thesis statement	"Everyone can get the most out of their smartphone through three ways:, organizing your life, eating better, and getting better sleep"
First speaking point	Organizing your life
• Supporting fact #1	
• Supporting fact #2	
• Supporting fact #3	
Second speaking point	Grocery shopping
• Supporting fact #1	
• Supporting fact #2	
• Supporting fact #3	

Last saved: July 15, 15

Third speaking point	Better sleep
• Supporting fact #1	
• Supporting fact #2	
• Supporting fact #3	
Conclusion	

Day 2 – Researching and developing the speech content

Research

Once you know the purpose of your speech, researching the speech will be much easier because you will have a better idea of what you are looking for to support your speech.

Here are the types of supporting material that you will want to look for (this is not a definitive list nor does every speech need all the supporting materials listed but this can help give you a few ideas on where to look). Pick and adapt the ones that will help achieve your speech's purpose. Later, I will talk about the sources that you may wish to look into in order to find the supporting material.

- Supporting material
  - Surprising facts / figures (e.g., there was a pie chart showing the reasons and corresponding percentages of people that leave Toastmasters. Two percent leave Toastmasters because of death – this does not mean that 98% of the people that join Toastmasters live forever)
  - A mystery, puzzle, enigma, etc. that leaves the audience wanting more
  - Anecdotes or stories that builds to a climax or surprise ending
  - Facts, figures, especially those that are quantitative (e.g., 8/10 doctors prefer Colgate, 45% of statistics are made up, etc.)
  - Quotes from celebrities, experts, etc.
  - Personal experience (either from yourself or from others)
  - Visuals (images, physical objects, etc.)

Sometimes I will go into a speech knowing everything that will be in the speech and other times, I will know nothing about the subject (but will want to learn and appear credible on the subject). The supporting materials will help you develop your speaking points and the supporting facts.

There are also a variety of sources that you can check to gain more knowledge on the subject of your speech:

- Sources
  - Google!
  - Wikipedia (I like using Wikipedia as a way to get a general understanding of the subject)
  - Citizendium (http://en.citizendium.org/) – a more strict version of Wikipedia that can be quoted and cited
  - Magazines (often times, finding magazines in that specific subject area will give you relevant articles)
  - Google Scholar (research papers)
  - Industry-specific websites (e.g., if you were looking for business topics, you may look at Harvard Business Review)

Last saved: July 15, 15

- o Brainyquote – a good source of quotes on a variety of subjects. Quotes are organized by the original person who first said it and by general subject matter so if you do not know the name of a particular expert in your subject, look through the quotes by the subject matter that is closest to the subject of your speech

- o Your local library (most often a very cheap or free way of finding resources – bringing books / magazines that you used as a source for your speech appears much more credible than saying that you found it on Google)

- o Friends / family / acquaintances you know that might know something about your speech subject

- o Infographics: http://dailyinfographic.com/

- o Your own personal experience (this can be a major source of information as the speech subject is often related to you as the speaker)

Development of your speech

My approach in trying to find material for my speech is to do as much research as I can without worrying about whether or not the information might be included in my speech or not. As I'm doing research online, I may use a tool like Evernote (www.evernote.com) to clip anything that I think might be useful (too much information can never be a bad thing and you never know what might be useful as you write your speech).

As I mentioned previously, the type of supporting material depends on your speech; however, as a general rule of thumb, I believe a well-researched speech will have at least three different types of supporting materials, from a variety of sources.

Once you have a variety of articles, quotes, statistics, stories, anecdotes, etc., for your speech, start to think about how your speech will progress from start to finish. To give you an idea, here is what I will think about depending on the general purpose of the speech:

- • Entertain

If you have a story that you are sharing, you may find that there are certain parts of your story that are not as entertaining – these areas would be a good place to insert an interesting fact, statistic or quote in order to make it more 'entertaining'. Sometimes the truth can be stranger than fiction, but there is nothing wrong with tweaking your story slightly (e.g., through exaggerating) to make it more entertaining. I certainly don't advocate lying but I have seen it used effectively in other speeches so that is also a possibility you can consider if nothing else works.

- • Inform

Are you trying to teach the audience something new? If you are following the sample structure that I have outlined during Day 1, you will need three speaking points. Ask yourself what three things can I tell the audience so that they will be knowledgeable about the subject (i.e., if I wanted to tell people about how great exercising can be, what three simple exercises can I share with the audience that would be easy to learn and provide great benefits to their health?). For my speech, I will be telling the audience about three applications that can help them in their daily life. Are these the only three applications that can help them? Certainly not. Are these three applications that anyone and everyone can use to help them in their lives? Yes, they are. Try to find points that everyone can relate to or agree with.

- • Persuade

If you are trying to persuade the audience on a point of view, what three speaking points/facts can I tell the audience that will help support my point of view? Does it make sense to provide some context/background (if so, this may be part of your introduction or your speaker's introduction)? Do certain facts rely on the validity of other facts? If so, certain speaking points may come first in your speech if it makes sense to do so.

- Motivate

If you are motivating your audience to take a step to improve themselves, how can your speaking points help convince the audience to take that step? When I create motivational speeches, I will generally follow this simple structure: I first explain to the audience what is currently wrong with what they are doing now (perhaps they're not exercising, etc.) and I explain the consequences of inaction. As part of my transition, I might identify various alternatives but I will focus on one particular alternative (which will be the focus of my speech). I will, as part of my second speaking point, explain the benefits of taking this small step. My third speaking point will then talk about what the next steps might be for those that take action. My speaking points will start off in a logical manner and then focus on the emotional state of mind of the audience (how will they feel at first, how will they feel as they take action and how will they feel after they have taken action).

Take a look at the structure of your speech, the general and specific purpose of your speech and all of the research you have found. Start to understand what your speaking points are and how the research you found can support your points. As you start to 'fit' your research into your speaking points, you will begin to understand what you might be missing and you can then focus your research on the specific supporting material you need.

End of day 2 checklist

Day 2 checklist (speech content)	
Question	**Action**
Does your speech have at least three types of supporting material? (Optional)	Depending on your speech (e.g., a humorous speech about your own personal experience), you may not need three types of supporting material. If you are having problems finding different sources, you may understand your speech better as you write it and find other sources that might be helpful.
Does your speech use a variety of sources for the content?	The more sources your speech uses, the more credibility it will have (just as an article's credibility is stronger with the more sources it references).
Do you have a specific type of audience that you are catering to?	If you are having trouble thinking about what kind of sources will have the most impact on your audience, think about your audience and what kind of facts / evidence / stories might convince them. If your audience is full of academics, research papers would be good reference material for your speech. If your audience is full of leaders, you may wish to incorporate your own stories of leadership into your speech.

Sample outline - Day 2

For Day 2, I have started to fill in the different speaking points. I am somewhat of a smartphone and tech enthusiast so I have a good idea of what kind of apps there are that would support my speaking points. As I started to fill in the different speaking points, I am reminded of the Apple ads that say, "There is an app for that" and think that might be a good speech title so I pencil it in for now and make a mental note to check and adjust it later if needed. The general structure that I have followed is to explain the real life situation of the scenario, then I will explain the typical challenges/problems that people face in those situations and then finally, I will talk about an app that can solve those challenges and the other benefits it provides.

General purpose of my speech:	Inform, but also persuade the audience in a way
Specific purpose of my speech:	How specifically they will be getting value out of their smartphone (through apps)
Speech title:	"There's an app for that"

Introduction	- Explain the strangest app that there can be (one that is an app on the iphone) – this will get the conversation started on apps and then focus the discussion on more useful apps
Thesis statement	"Everyone can get the most out of their smartphone through three ways:, organizing your life, eating better, and getting better sleep"
First speaking point	Organizing your life
• Supporting fact #1	Explain why organizing your life is important
• Supporting fact #2	Explain what the challenges are in organizing your life
• Supporting fact #3	Application to organize life: Evernote (note taking, lists, etc.)
Second speaking point	Grocery shopping
• Supporting fact #1	Explain how much grocery shopping we do and how we can make it better
• Supporting fact #2	Explain what are the challenges / problems / issues we face when we go grocery shopping

• Supporting fact #3	Application to get coupons and to organize shopping: Checkout 51, WunderList. (to create lists)
Third speaking point	Better sleep
• Supporting fact #1	Explain the benefits of sleep (how much sleep we need, how much sleep the average busy person gets) – this is a good place for statistics
• Supporting fact #2	Explain the challenges of getting a good night's rest
• Supporting fact #3	Application to track your sleep: Sleep as Android (Android) / Sleep Cycle (iphone) - fitbit
Conclusion	- Recap the applications covered and the benefits of using the applications - Reiterate the smartphone numbers again - Explain that there are many more applications that can be used to get more value out of the smartphone (just google what you want to do with your smartphone to find apps) - End with "There's an app for that"

Day 3 – Transitions and memorizing your speech

Transitions

After day 2, we have developed the outline of the speech and we can start to fill in the details of what exactly we want to say. Normally, from the outline, I will start to practice my speech, figure out what I would like to talk about and time myself to ensure that I am under the time limit if there is one; however, for illustrative purposes, I will write out the speech word for word and in the later days, highlight specific areas for body language, vocal variety, etc.

Here again is the outline that we developed after Day 2 (the outline is bolded so that you can see where I have started to fill in the speech):

There's an app for that

Introduction (explain some strange apps, explain what an app is, explain that there are useful apps)

Do you want to make fart sounds when your boss sits down? Do you want to prove to your friends that you are rich? Do you want to prank your friends with a phone that looks like it is cracked? There's an app for that. There are over a million apps on each of the major platforms: Apple and Android. If you have ever wished that you could do something with your smartphone, it most like already exists! What I want to talk about today isn't the strange applications however; **today, I will tell you how you can get more value out of your smartphone in three different areas of your life: organization, grocery shopping and sleeping.**

The first way you can get more from your smartphone is to become more organized. How many of you have mountains and mountains of paper at home that you can't seem to make yourself throw away? It may be receipts, letters from the bank, random notes that you have jotted down, user manuals from things that you have bought but whatever it is, it is either strewn about on your table or filed away somewhere that you have to manage. You may have thought: there must be a better way to manage all this paper!

And there is! It's called Evernote! Evernote labels itself as your second brain. It is a note taking application that can capture recordings, video, audio, images and any notes that you have. It is the perfect application to digitize your paper so that 1) you do not have to keep stacks of paper around and 2) tag it so that you can find it later if needed. Organize all of your paper using your smartphone.

The second way you can get more from you smartphone is during grocery shopping. How many of you already use your smartphone when grocery shopping? How do you use it? *(Note: asking for audience interaction can be a challenge - I am interested in seeing if people use it already to search for coupons or compile shopping lists and if they do, then I can talk about it briefly and move on to the next subject.)* Did you know that you can use it to save money? In the past, we used to cut out coupons from magazines and newspapers to save money on different grocery items; now, you can save money using your phone! Checkout 51 is an application that I use which lists the coupons you can use to save money. If you purchase any items eligible for coupons, all you have to do is snap a picture of the receipt and the money builds up on your account. Once it reaches $20, you can request a cheque that will be sent to your home. No more cutting out coupons, no more forgetting them when you go out to shop. Save money using your smartphone.

Last saved: July 15, 15

The third and final way you can use your smartphone is when you sleep. Sleep is quite a problem for those of us that lead busy lives. We can't seem to get enough of it and we can't seem to get quality sleep either. Did you know that your smartphone can help you sleep better? There are applications on the phone that will track how many hours you slept, how many hours of deep sleep you had and can even gently wake you up at the optimal time based on your movements and your sleep cycles. I use an application called Sleep as Android which will calculate how many hours of sleep you had, how many cycles of deep sleep you went through and will track how well you have slept over weeks or months if you are interested in that kind of data. Get better sleep using your smartphone!

I have shown you how you can use your smartphone in three different areas of your life: using Evernote to get rid of paper, using Checkout 51 to save money on groceries and using Sleep as Android to sleep better. There are a huge number of applications out there that can help you with any problems you may face – all you have to do the next time you have an issue is search for the problem that you have with 'app' and even you might say, "There's an app for that".

After writing out the whole speech, I give the speech a one-over to make sure that everything follows in a logical manner. I identify various areas for transitions and make sure that I am using the appropriate transitions in those places to help the audience understand (you can see the transitions and how I adjusted in the sample outline – Day 3 at the end of Day 3). Although it is hard to do since you are so intimately involved in your speech, you have to try to read and listen to your speech as if you have never heard it before. In my speech above, I have highlighted in light blue, the areas where I think the transitions could be stronger. I also review the word count (723 words) – assuming that I speak about 120 words per minute, that means that my speech will be about 6 minutes; however, I will go through my speech a few times just to make sure as the word count does not account for pauses (both intentional and unintentional) as you speak. Also, when you are nervous (as many people are when they get up in front of people to speak), you will speak faster but again, practice until you feel you have the time just right. My personal rule of thumb is to practice until you can speak slightly past the bare minimum; this way, you have some flexibility if you go over your practiced time limit for pauses and any interruptions if they were to occur from the audience. It is always easier to say a few more things to reach a specific time limit if you have to then it is to cut down on the material you already have because you are way over time.

Memorizing your speech

When I first started memorizing speeches, I memorized the whole speech word for word. I memorized through repetition and it worked for me for a while. Except one time where I horribly bombed!

I remember the day like it was yesterday – I was preparing a Toast where I was speaking in tribute of a member of Toastmasters who had recently completed some great achievements. I got up to my 2nd speaking point and then I completely blanked. I tried all of my techniques to jog my memory to get back on track but it was not working! I even said aloud "Oh no, this is not good" <- please do not do this in your own speech. I eventually fumbled my way through the 2nd speaking point, then ended up blanking slightly on the 3rd speaking point and my conclusion was not as strong as it could have been. Needless to say, it was a speech that I wished I could have a do-over on.

It's funny that when things are working, you do not think about other methods or ways to improve. I thought that this method of memorizing the speech word for word was fine but I realized, only too late, that there were actually superior methods for memorizing speeches. The technique that I now use to memorize speeches is to remember general ideas and then practice communicating those ideas in my own words as much as I can before the actual speech. I would be lying if I said that after switching over to this technique, I have not had memory slips since but with this technique, I am less reliant on notes and better suited to adapt to minor adjustments in my speech (for example, if I receive new information from an audience member or if the host suddenly decides to cut my speech by 2 minutes, etc.). This technique also allows me to not rely on specific words or sentences (sometimes when speakers memorize things word for word and they veer from the script, they lose their place because their memory is so reliant on staying to the script in that specific order) and allows me to adjust as necessary – if I completely blank out but still know the general idea, I can at least salvage that speaking point (or the speech if it goes terribly wrong) and finish the speech. Remember, the audience has no idea what you are going to say so as long as you do not let them know that you have forgotten your speech, they will think that this was planned all along.

Memorization technique

The following table shows how I have broken down the components of my speech into 'general' ideas. These are the ideas that I memorize. While practicing, I will expand on these ideas and practice the expansion (without worrying about whether I say the same thing each time) in order to get the wording and timing just right.

Another plus with breaking down the components of your speech is that you can write these ideas in large font on cue cards; if you do forget your speech, you can quickly refer to your cue cards for these general ideas and get back on track right away. If you typed out your speech word for word, it would take time to find where you currently are in the script and that time is time not spent connecting with the audience through eye contact.

Try not to make more work for yourself – use the outline that you have created during Day 2 to help you with your 'general' ideas and adjust as needed, as you may have changed your speech over Day 3.

Component of the speech	Speech outline	Memorization notes
Introduction	Explain the strangest app that there can be (there's an app on the iphone that is) – this will get the conversation started on apps and then focus the discussion on more useful apps	Strange apps
Thesis statement	"Everyone can get the most out of their smartphone through three ways:, organizing your life, eating better, and getting better sleep"	Useful apps – organization, grocery shopping, sleeping
First speaking point	Organizing your life	Organizing your life
• Supporting fact #1	Explain why organizing your life is important	Scenario (paper)
• Supporting fact #2	Explain what are the challenges in organizing your life	Challenges of physical paper

• Supporting fact #3	Application to organize life: Evernote (note taking, lists, etc.)	App (Evernote)
Second speaking point	Grocery shopping	Grocery shopping
• Supporting fact #1	Explain how much grocery shopping we do and how we can make it better	Scenario (coupons)
• Supporting fact #2	Explain what are the challenges / problems / issues we face when we go grocery shopping	Challenges of coupons
• Supporting fact #3	Application to get coupons and to organize shopping: Checkout 51, WunderList (to create lists)	App (Checkout 51)
Third speaking point	Better sleep	Better sleep
• Supporting fact #1	Explain the benefits of sleep (how much sleep we need, how much sleep the average busy person gets) – this is a good place for statistics	Scenario (better sleep)
• Supporting fact #2	Explain the challenges of getting a good night's rest	Challenges of sleep
• Supporting fact #3	Application to track your sleep: Sleep as Android (Android) / Sleep Cycle (iphone) - fitbit	App (Sleep as Android)
Conclusion	- Recap the applications covered and the benefits of using the applications - Reiterate the smartphone numbers again - Explain that there are many more applications that can be used to get more value out of the smartphone (just google what you want to do with your smartphone to find apps) - End with "There's an app for that"	- Recap - How can the audience find apps that are useful to them? - "There's an app for that"

End of day 3 checklist

Question	Action
Have you started to map the research you have done to the different components of your speech?	Use your outline as a guide to help you figure out what research can be used to support your speaking points.
Do you have areas in your speech that needs to be fleshed out more?	Again, using your outline, you can identify areas in your speech where you need to do more research.
Do you have appropriate transitions in each of your speaking points?	Take one of the three speaking points aside and read it on its own. Does it make sense? Can the audience follow your speaking point and its supporting facts? Do this for each of your speaking points.
Do you have appropriate transitions between your speaking points (i.e., from the intro to speaking point #1, between speaking points, and then from speaking point #3 to your conclusion)?	Read through your whole speech, noting the specific areas and making sure the general ideas logically flow from one idea to the next.
Have you broken down your speech into smaller, easy-to-memorize components?	Use the outline you developed during Day 2 to help you create easy-to-memorize notes for your speech.
Can you rearrange your speaking points on the fly without having to spend extra time memorizing?	If yes, you are well on your way of knowing your speech rather than memorizing your speech word for word.

Sample outline – Day 3

For Day 3, I have populated the outline with the whole speech developed in the Transitions section. I have also adjusted the speech for transitions and have highlighted all of the transitions below.

Tip: Use your 'down' time wisely. If you have a few minutes, try quizzing yourself by picking one component of your speech and only talking about that component (e.g., for this speech, I might practice the scenario of grocery shopping so that I can get the wording right). This has the added benefit of helping you practice for when you get 'stuck' because you couldn't remember the exact wording you used or if you rearranged your speech at the last minute.

Introduction	Do you want to make fart sounds when your boss sits down? Do you want to prove to your friends that you are rich? Do you want to prank your friends with a phone that looks like it is cracked? There's an app for that. There are over a million apps on each of the major platforms: Apple and Android. If you have ever wished that you could do something with your smartphone, it most like already exists!
Thesis statement	What I want to talk about today aren't the strange applications however; today, I will tell you how you can get more value out of your smartphone in three different areas of your life: organization, grocery shopping and sleeping.
First speaking point	The first way you can get more from your smartphone is to become more organized.
• Supporting fact #1	I have a problem at home and work that I hope you can relate to: how many of you have mountains and mountains of paper on your desk that you can't seem to make yourself throw away? It may be receipts, letters from the bank, random notes that you have jotted down, user manuals from things that you have bought but whatever it is, it is either strewn about on your table or filed away somewhere that you have to manage. You may have thought: there must be a better way to manage all this paper!
• Supporting fact #2	
• Supporting fact #3	And there is! It's called Evernote! Evernote labels itself as your second brain. It is a note taking application that can capture recordings, video, audio, images and any notes that you have. It is the perfect application to digitize your paper so that 1) you do not have to keep stacks of paper around and 2) tag it so that you can find it later if needed. Organize all of your paper using your smartphone.
Second speaking point	The second way you can get more from you smartphone is during grocery shopping.
• Supporting fact #1	How many of you already use your smartphone when grocery shopping? How do you use it? *(Note: asking for audience interaction can be a challenge - I am interested in seeing if people use it already to search for coupons or compile shopping lists and if they do, then I can talk about it briefly and move on to*

• Supporting fact #2	*the next subject).* Did you know that you can use it to save money? In the past, we used to cut out coupons from magazines and newspapers to save money on different grocery items; now, you can save money using your phone! Checkout 51 is an application that I use which lists the coupons you can use to save money. If you purchase any items eligible for coupons, all you have to do is
• Supporting fact #3	snap a picture of the receipt and the money builds up on your account. Once it reaches $20, you can request a cheque that will be sent to your home. No more cutting out coupons, no more forgetting them when you go out to shop. Save money using your smartphone.
Third speaking point	The third and final way you can use your smartphone is when you sleep.
• Supporting fact #1	Sleep is quite a problem for those of us that lead busy lives. We can't seem to get enough of it and we can't seem to get quality sleep either. How many of you feel like you don't get enough sleep or enough quality sleep? Did you know that your smartphone can help you sleep better? There are applications on the
• Supporting fact #2	phone that will track how many hours you slept, how many hours of deep sleep you had and can even gently wake you up at the optimal time based on your movements and your sleep cycles. I use an application called Sleep as Android which will calculate how many hours of sleep you had, the quality of your
• Supporting fact #3	sleep and how well you have slept over weeks or months if you are interested in that kind of data. This data will help you identify optimal times for sleep, optimal length of sleep time and other ways to get better sleep – all through using your smartphone!
Conclusion	I have shown you how you can use your smartphone in three different areas of your life: using Evernote to get rid of paper, using Checkout 51 to save money on groceries and using Sleep as Android to sleep better. There are a huge number of applications out there that can help you with any problems you face – all you have to do the next time you face a problem is search for the problem that you have with 'app' and even you might say, "There's an app for that".

Day 4 - Understanding and incorporating body language

When I first started speaking and thinking about how to incorporate body language into my speech, I had a hard time trying to incorporate something that just wasn't 'me'. I am an introvert by nature and not one to stand out by any means so I thought that using wide sweeping arms or large exaggerated movements would be strange because it's not something that I would normally do. Over my years of speaking, my body language has not changed drastically but I have improved my body language through my own style. It might not be as impressive as other speakers but it helps me get my message across and I feel that it is natural.

In terms of body language that you can use to enhance your speech, there are a ton of techniques that you can use. I cannot cover them all, but I can give you a good sample to think about and choose from to incorporate into your speech.

Note: there are many different types of body language you can incorporate in your speech and you can even use the same type of body language to emphasize different parts of your speech. If you are interested in even more things that you can do with your body - look on Youtube and search for "improv" or "whose line is it anyway" and watch how the actors physically use their bodies to create punch lines. The body language they use is not just for humour either! As always, experimentation is a big part of finding out what is natural for you, what works for you and other ways you can use body language to emphasize different parts of your speech.

Body language examples

These are all things that I have done in my speeches in the past and I have used them to great effect (whether the audience knew about them or not).

Movement around the room

Body language	How you can use it to emphasize your speech
Moving from one side of the room / podium / speaking area to another	• Moving from one topic to another, e.g., any transitions that you might want to use in your speech • Talking about opposite sides of a controversial topic (i.e., you can combine this with the transition sentence 'on the one hand' and then move to the other side of the room when you say 'on the other hand')

Body language	How you can use it to emphasize your speech
Moving from the back of the speaking area to the front (can be gradual, can be one large step)	• If gradually moving forwards: you can use it to talk about different points that are more and more important to your speech • If gradually moving forwards: you can use it as a way to build excitement to the climax of your story (then walking backwards, you can use it to conclude / resolve your story) • If one large step forwards: you can use it to emphasize the crux or the most important point of your speech • If one large step backwards: you can use this to show 'surprise' or 'shock' in your speech or you can use it to emphasize a bad idea or a problem in your speech. (e.g., WHAT? (step back) You want to pour money into a company called Google?)
Crouching down on one knee	• You can use this to show 'exhaustion', combined with breathing heavily but it's also a unique way of grabbing your audience's attention • You can also use this to show hardships in a story or speech - talk about how everything was good in the beginning, hardships (crouch down) and then after solving them, standing up to show that you have conquered your hardship
Lying down on the ground	• I have used this at the beginning of my speech to grab everyone's attention (at the time of my speech, everybody was sitting in tables arranged in a 'U' and I was lying down in the middle of the room so everyone had to stand up to see what I was doing). This is a good way to begin speeches where there is a 'beginning' (I started my day in bed, I started my business from the ground up, etc.).

There are so many things that you can do with your hands during your speech (and some of them seem quite obvious) but one of the worst things that you could do with your hands is portraying nervousness somehow through:

- Wringing your hands
- Bringing a clicky pen up and clicking nervously (I did this! It was awful)
- Putting your hands in your pockets

This brings up another reason why you should be memorizing your speech. If you have a script that you bring up with you to the stage / podium / lectern, it can severely limit the ways your hands can move about if you have to hold on to the script for most of your speech.

Body language	How you can use it to emphasize your speech
Arms raised above your head in a 'V' position	• The power pose (search for Amy Cuddy on Youtube / Ted Talks) can help give you confidence before a speech and it can also show power or triumph during your speech (e.g., after you finished a marathon or successfully made a good impression with your in-laws)
Arms closed around your body and your whole body is scrunched to become as small as possible	• This can be used to show fear or weakness in a speech (e.g., you are about to enter a cave or you are about to approach someone at the bar)
Arms spread out as wide as possible	• Used to emphasize something BIG (e.g., I was in BIG trouble, the spider was this HUGE)
Hands held together as close as possible in front of your body (but not touching) OR Fingers held together as close as possible in front of your body (but not touching)	• Used to emphasize something SMALL (e.g., I had a SMALL problem, the recipe required only a pinch of salt)
Any number of fingers up	• Can be used to outline different points (First, ..., Second,... Third,..., etc.) • "I have three reasons why I think this is the case"

Body language	How you can use it to emphasize your speech
Shrugging of your shoulders and holding your hands to the sides, palms face up	• You can use this to emphasize confusion (e.g., I had no idea what to do next, How did I know that she was going to do that?) • Having open palms shows innocence or honesty (as in "I didn't steal the cookies")
Pushing your shoulders back and baring your chest	• Shows bravado (e.g., I didn't want to enter the cave but when I knew my cat was inside, I couldn't help but feel brave)
Holding your arms open (as if about to hug someone)	• Shows welcoming / embracing (e.g., you can use this to embrace an idea or view point that you were not convinced of before – "And finally, I understood (hold arms open) and I let the concept embrace me)
Holding your hands over your heart	• Shows that something is precious to you (e.g., when you are talking about your child, or when you are talking about your prized possession)

Head / face

When people watch you speak, they are primarily looking at your face to see how you yourself are reacting to your own speech. If you are talking about something exciting, but your face shows boredom, the audience will be confused as to what kind of message you are trying to deliver to them. The audience will watch your face for cues on how to take specific things in your speech (if you show passion or excitement, they will similarly be more passionate and excited for your speech) and therefore, it is important to understand what kind of mood you will want to portray to the audience and make sure that it aligns with your speech (or, if it does not align, why not?).

Body language	How you can use it to emphasize your speech
Raise both eye brows	• Can show 'surprise' • Raising both eye brows twice can imply certain things. It's especially fun when you raise your eye brows twice to strangers (friends and acquaintances as well).

Body language	How you can use it to emphasize your speech
Close your eyes and shake your head in your hand	• Can show that something is a bad idea (e.g., "I watched my friend sneak onto the stage and thought to myself (close your eyes and shake your head), this was an awful idea")
Smile	The amount of time you smile can imply different things: • A short smile can portray confidence, a plan that you have, something humorous • A longer smile (one that turns bigger and bigger) can mean something going on that someone doesn't know (e.g., My friend was about to try a Rocky Mountain Oyster because he loves seafood (long smile))
Frown	• You can use a frown to emphasize something that you don't like or something that you don't agree with (e.g., the mayor wanted to increase the funding for public transit (frown) yet with decreasing ridership, the numbers did not support this increase in funding)
Eyes looking from side to side	• You can use this as a way to appear suspicious or that you do not want to get 'caught' (e.g., I looked around before stealing the keys from my boss' desk)

Incorporating body language into your speech

These examples will help give you ideas on how you can incorporate body language into your speech, but I also recognize that not everyone will have the experience to incorporate different body language into their speech right away. Therefore, I am proposing a gradual incorporation of developing the body language that you use in your speech:

1. Do not worry about incorporating any body language into your speech at first. While you practice your speech, take into account the body language that you use naturally (we all do something naturally whether its hand gestures, moving around, expressions on our face – a mirror would be a good place to practice as awkward as it might be to watch yourself speak)

2. Another good way of finding your natural body language is to notice what you do the next time you are speaking to someone you are extremely comfortable with (your friend, parent, etc.) or when you are talking about something you are very passionate about.

3. There are some things that you might do as nervous tics. Examples of these nervous tics could be:

   - Wringing or clasping your hands
   - Pacing back and forth
   - Shifting your weight to and from one leg to the other
   - Tightly gripping paper, props, the lectern or the podium

   These tics are some of the more common things that I see but look for anything that you do not do purposefully and that you do an excessive amount of.

4. As you gradually do more speeches and gain more confidence in your public speaking abilities, you will start to reduce the number of nervous tics that you might have had previously and begin to use body language more purposefully in your speech. Start with the power pose and walking confidently up to the speaking area when called upon. Before speaking with your audience, smile. At the end of your speech, smile. These simple and small tips can help to increase your confidence in your speaking ability and show the audience that you are confident in your speech as well.

5. As you do more and more speeches, you can start to incorporate more body language into your speeches to make your speech more impactful and to emphasize different points in your speech. Use the examples as a guide, matching what you are trying to accomplish with the body language that you can use to emphasize your goal. I encourage you to either try out one new body language technique in a speech, get some feedback from your friends or people in the audience and then try out another technique. Learn what was done well, and keep the things that made your speech more effective.

End of day 4 checklist

Day 4 checklist (body language)	
Question	**Action**
What body language do you naturally exhibit?	When you speak passionately about a subject or when you are speaking to friends, what kind of body language do you use, if any?
Do you have any nervous tics in terms of body language? Do you do anything excessive with your body that you don't normally do when speaking?	There is a difference between nervous body language and 'purposeful' body language. Nervous tics will give your audience the sense that you are nervous and then they might question why you are nervous (are you not confident about your speech? Are you not an expert about your subject?). Purposeful body language will align to and emphasize the points in your speech and help engrain the message into your audience's minds.
Do you have specific points in your speech that can be emphasized through body language?	There are most likely specific points in your speech that are easier to emphasize through body language than other points. You will get a better idea of what speaking points can be emphasized through body language as you do more public speaking but as you can tell through the examples provided, there are many opportunities for incorporating body language into your speech.
Do you portray confidence throughout your speech?	Walking confidently up to the speaking area and smiling throughout your speech will give your audience a sense of confidence in you and your speech.
Are you trying out new body language techniques in your speech?	Practice until you can get your body language and words in sync (i.e., do you know what you are going to say and how your body will move?)

Sample outline - Day 4

For Day 4, I have listed out sample body language that I would use if I were to deliver this speech with the relevant text highlighted. In this way, you can start to understand where in your speech you might be able to use body language to emphasize the points in your speech.

Speech component	Speech	Body language
Introduction	Do you want to make fart sounds when your boss sits down? Do you want to prove to your friends that you are rich? Do you want to prank your friends with a phone that looks like it is cracked? There's an app for that. There are over a million apps on each of the major platforms: Apple and Android. If you have ever wished that you could do something with your smartphone, it most like already exists!	I believe this is a good opportunity to emphasize different apps on your smartphone and actually do these things through an app (however, I think the time it takes to demonstrate and switch over to another app might mean you would have to cut it down to 2 examples). There is probably a fart app and there is a cracked phone screen prank app so I will use those 2 as examples.

Do you want to make fart sounds when your boss sits down? (make a fart noise on your phone)

Do you want to pretend that you cracked your friend's smartphone? (show the cracked screen on your own smartphone) |
Thesis statement	What I want to talk about today aren't the strange applications however; today, I will tell you how you can get more value out of your smartphone in three different areas of your life: organization, grocery shopping and sleeping.	As you say, "Three different areas of your life"- hold up three fingers. As you discuss the three points, hold up the corresponding number of fingers, e.g., 1, organization, 2, grocery shopping and finally 3, sleeping.
First speaking point	The first way you can get more from your smartphone is to become more organized.	
• Supporting fact #1	I have a problem at home and work that I hope you can relate to: how many of you have mountains and mountains of paper on your desk that you can't seem to make yourself throw	"Mountains and mountains of paper on your desk that you can't seem to make yourself throw away" (scrunch up some paper and try to throw it away but think better of it)

• Supporting fact #2	away? It may be receipts, letters from the bank, random notes that you have jotted down, user manuals from things that you have bought but whatever it is,	
• Supporting fact #3	it is either strewn about on your table or filed away somewhere that you have to manage. You may have thought: there must be a better way to manage all this paper! And there is! It's called Evernote! Evernote labels itself as your second brain. It is a note taking application that can capture recordings, video, audio, images and any notes that you have. It is the perfect application to digitize your paper so that 1) you do not have to keep stacks of paper around and 2) tag it so that you can find it later if needed. Organize all of your paper using your smartphone.	After saying "Organize all of your paper using your smartphone", you can ad-lib a little bit and say something like "in fact, earlier today, I reminded myself to" (look down at your smartphone) "deliver a speech" In the air with your finger, make a check "Check!" This would be an easy way to add a little bit of humour to your speech. Even better may be to record you saying, "deliver a speech at <fill in the blank>" and then say "Check!"
Second speaking point	The second way you can get more from you smartphone is during grocery shopping.	
• Supporting fact #1	How many of you already use your smartphone when grocery shopping? How do you use it? Did you know that you can use it to save money? In the past, we used to cut out coupons from magazines and newspapers to	Remember to pause after saying "How do you use it". Speakers can sometimes have rhetorical questions that do not need answers but if you are expecting audience feedback then you will have to let the audience know.
• Supporting fact #2		

• Supporting fact #3	coupons, no more forgetting them when you go out to shop. Save money using your smartphone.	smartphone (or say it yourself).
Third speaking point	The third and final way you can use your smartphone is when you sleep.	
• Supporting fact #1 • Supporting fact #2 • Supporting fact #3	Sleep is quite a problem for those of us that lead busy lives. We can't seem to get enough of it and we can't seem to get quality sleep either. How many of you feel like you don't get enough sleep or enough quality sleep? Did you know that your smartphone can help you sleep better? There are applications on the phone that will track how many hours you slept, how many hours of deep sleep you had and can even gently wake you up at the optimal time based on your movements and your sleep cycles. I use an application called Sleep as Android which will calculate how many hours of sleep you had, the quality of your sleep and how well you have slept over weeks or months if you are interested in that kind of data. This data will help you identify optimal times for sleep, optimal length of sleep time and other ways to get better sleep – all through using your smartphone!	"How many of you feel like you don't get enough sleep or enough quality sleep?" - raise your hand at the same time to give your audience the cue to raise their hands if they agree Perhaps this is a good place to pull out your smartphone and hold it up in the air to showcase it.

| Conclusion | I have showed you how you can use your smartphone in three different areas of your life: using Evernote to get rid of paper, using Checkout 51 to save money on groceries and using Sleep as Android to sleep better. There are a huge number of applications out there that can help you with any problems you face – all you have to do the next time you have a problem is search for the problem that you have with 'app' and even you might say "there's an app for that". | As you conclude your speech "...and even you might say" (hold up your smartphone) "there's an app for that" |

Day 5 - Understanding how to use your voice

Similar to incorporating body language, when I first learned about how to use my voice for maximum impact during my speech, I immediately thought of Robin Williams and Jim Carey and all of the impressions and bits that they do in a variety of scenarios. Could I be like Robin Williams or Jim Carey? Not a chance!

However, I started learning about all of the different ways that you can use your voice and it wasn't just about doing voice impressions – there were a variety of ways that you could use your voice for emphasis that did not involve impersonating a celebrity or faking an accent. These ways include:

- Volume (how loud or soft you speak)
- Pace (how fast or slow you speak)
- Breathing / Pauses (similar to body language but achieved through your voice instead)
- Enunciation (and a component of that which is pronunciation)
- Pitch (a happy or excited voice is different than a sad or somber voice)

Vocal variety in action (examples)

I understand how important it can be to have examples so I have listed out the various vocal variety techniques and provided samples of those techniques in action. Please note that these are not hard and fast rules or examples; these are mainly used to show you how you can use these techniques in your own speech.

Vocal technique	Example of vocal technique in action
Volume	Loud (used to show passion or excitement): "How COOL is the new iphone?"
	Soft (used to show seriousness, sadness): "I slowly walked up to the coffin to look into my grandfather's face and tried to remember as many happy memories as I could"
	Note: Volume is a great way to contrast different parts of a speech; however, my piano teacher once taught me that in order to show this contrast, you may have to exaggerate the louds so that people can still hear the softs. The audience may not be able to hear your 'soft' voice so if you increase the volume of your normal voice, you will not have to soften your normal voice as much. This should also be considered if there is background noise in the room you are speaking in (like the white noise from an exhaust fan or a heater)

Vocal technique	Example of vocal technique in action
Pace	Fast (used to show excitement in your speech): "and then he flung open the door, jumped out of the house and started yelling 'bloody murder' at the top of his lungs" Slow (used to show a careful approach or in conjunction with softness, can be used to show seriousness / sadness): "He trudged out from the casino after losing all of his money betting on black on the roulette table"
Breathing / Pauses	This can be used in conjunction with the pause in order to emphasize the importance of something you are going to say / what you have just said "That's when she said (breathe in) 'I'm leaving you'"
Enunciation / pronunciation	English is a complex language and one of the complexities of English is that there are words / phrases that sound the same when said aloud (bare, bear). There are also words and phrases that sound similar but are not exactly the same (electrical vs. electoral). At times, when I want to make sure that I get a particular term, concept or complex word right, I will make sure to slow down and enunciate; if I do not do this, I know that I would speed up as that is what people normally do when they are nervous and this results in a greater chance of fumbling over the word. As an example, I have slowed down my speech when saying large, very complex words: "Today, I am going to talk about what DNA or" (slow down to a pace that is unnaturally slow) "de-oxy-ribo-nucleic- acid" "I believe that we all could benefit from learning about MRSA" or (slow down!) "Methicillin-resistant, staphylococcus aureus"

Vocal technique	Example of vocal technique in action
Pitch	An easy way for me to remember what pitch is and why to include it in a speech is to think of a salesman delivering a sales pitch. Any salesman that truly believes in the product they are selling will have passion and excitement in their voice and the pitch of their voice may even be slightly higher due to their excitement (think of guys squealing in excitement for the latest car or gadget).
	Excited voice (high pitched): "I am going to show you an incredible app for your phone that will predict the stock market for you"
	Serious voice (low pitched): "The professor's speech stopped time itself"

Incorporating vocal variety into your speech

Similar to incorporating body language into your speech, I recognize that people reading this e-book will have a variety of speaking backgrounds and it can be tough to incorporate vocal variety into your speech when that is something you do not normally do when speaking to friends or family. I encourage you to take an approach similar to incorporating body language in your speech (the outline is almost the same as for body language):

1. Do not worry about incorporating any vocal variety into your speech at first. While you practice your speech, take into account the vocal variety that you use naturally (if possible, record yourself saying your speech. As you read, you will notice where you use different vocal variety techniques). Remember that your audience can read into your voice so if you are excited, the audience will also feel excited.

2. There are some things that you might do as nervous tics. Examples of these nervous tics could be:

    - Breathing heavily, gasps

    - Dry lips (and therefore, lip smacking – you can hear this most commonly before starting a sentence)

    - Gulping constantly (due to a dry throat)

    - A monotone voice that does not change pitch, pace or volume

    These tics are some of the more common tics that I see but look for anything that you do not do purposefully and that you do an excessive amount of.

3. As you gradually do more speeches and gain more confidence in your public speaking abilities, you will start to reduce the number of nervous tics that you might have had previously and begin to use vocal variety more purposefully in your speech. I myself try not to go overboard with vocal variety because at some point, it can be a little too much. Think of it like salt in

Last saved: July 15, 15

your food, use a bit of salt for taste but don't pile it on – you want the audience to focus on your speech and its contents, not on the loud and soft parts of your speech.

4. Finally, as you start to understand what techniques you can use with the different parts of your speech, you can start to experiment with vocal variety to see what might be effective with the audience (e.g., instead of speaking loudly to catch the audience's attention, try speaking softly and then ramping up in volume). It is important not to try out new techniques that you have not used before for an important speech – try it out in a safe setting, get some feedback and then use it.

Day 5 checklist (vocal variety)	
<u>Question</u>	<u>Action</u>
What kind of natural vocal variety techniques do you already use?	Try recording yourself saying a variety of different things: an article from your favourite magazine, a letter from a friend, a research paper you did not enjoy, etc. Noting down the different ways your voice changed will give you a nice 'baseline' of what techniques are already in your repertoire.
Do you have any nervous tics in terms of your vocal variety? Do you do anything excessive with your voice (or mouth) that you do not normally do when speaking?	Look at the examples in Step 2 of incorporating your vocal variety for the most common nervous tics with your voice / mouth. Be aware of them when you are speaking and try to mitigate them as much as possible (by practicing, having confidence in your speech and taking a sip of water before you speak, etc.)

Question	Action
Do you feel like you do not have good vocal variety? Do you feel like uncomfortable incorporating vocal variety techniques into your speech?	You are capable of all the vocal variety techniques I have listed above (and more) and I can tell you that it is perfectly normal to feel uncomfortable at first. Speaking is in part, a show, an act – it can be funny sometimes to see how different people are when they speak in front of an audience and when they speak to you one-on-one. Do what you feel is comfortable and then slowly start to expand and do more things that you may not be comfortable with.

Practice different vocal variety techniques on one sentence to start and notice how it changes the meaning of the sentence:

Volume:

- I HAD a bike.
- I had A bike.
- I had a BIKE.

Pace:

- (Fast) I had a bike.
- (Slow) I had a bike.

Pitch:

- (Excited) I had a bike.
- (Sad) I had a bike (notice that this may be similar to the slow pace example)

Once you understand how vocal variety can change or emphasize the meaning of the words or sentences you say, all you have to do is figure out what you want to convey to the audience for a particular sentence and use the appropriate technique.

Sample outline - Day 5

For Day 5, similar to Day 4's outline, I have written down the speech and highlighted the specific areas that I believe you can use vocal variety to enhance the speech. I explain exactly what I would do in the right-most column and hopefully this serves as a good example of how you might incorporate vocal variety into your own speech.

Note: Much of the vocal variety that I will talk about are places where I can see an opportunity for vocal variety – this does not mean that the list is complete or that you have to use a specific vocal variety for a specific effect. The outline serves as a teaching example.

Speech component	Speech	Vocal variety
Introduction	Do you want to make fart sounds when your boss sits down? Do you want to prove to your friends that you are rich? Do you want to prank your friends with a phone that looks like it is cracked? There's an app for that. There are over a million apps on each of the major platforms: Apple and Android. If you have ever wished that you could do something with your smartphone, it most like already exists!	The highlighted text makes me think of a salesman / t.v. infomercial that tries to pitch something to you. This would be a good place to speak at a fast pace to simulate this idea (this speech is about 'selling' the idea of these apps after all).
Thesis statement	What I want to talk about today aren't the strange applications however; today, I will tell you how you can get more value out of your smartphone in three different areas of your life: organization, grocery shopping and sleeping.	When I am telling the audience what I will be talking about, I slow down and pause to make sure the audience understands exactly what I will be talking about. "three different areas of your life: organization *pause*, grocery shopping *pause*, and sleeping)
First speaking point	The first way you can get more from your smartphone is to become more organized.	Again, slowed down so that the audience can follow along easily.
• Supporting fact #1	I have a problem at home and work that I hope you can relate to: how many of you have mountains and mountains of paper on your desk that you can't seem to make yourself throw away? It may be receipts, letters from the bank, random notes that	

• Supporting fact #2	you have jotted down,		
	user manuals from things that you have bought but whatever it is, it is either strewn about on your		
• Supporting fact #3	table or filed away somewhere that you have to manage. You may have thought: there must be a better way to manage all this paper!	"there must be a better way to manage all this paper!" (rising up in volume to show frustration)	
	And there is! It's called Evernote! Evernote labels itself as your second brain. It is a note taking application that can capture recordings, video, audio, images and any notes that you have. It is the perfect application to digitize your paper so that 1) you do not have to keep stacks of paper around and 2) tag it so that you can find it later if needed. Organize all of your paper using your smartphone.	"And there is!" (I will say this sentence at a similar volume to the previous sentence but I think this is a good place to experiment with different volumes – for example, I think a soft volume would work as well because the contrast would grab people's attention). Slightly slow in pace when saying "Organize" to match the beginning of your first speaking point and to leave the idea of "organize" in the audience's mind.	
Second speaking point	The second way you can get more from you smartphone is during grocery shopping.	Same as above, slow down when saying grocery shopping to help your audience follow along with your speech.	
• Supporting fact #1	How many of you already use your smartphone when grocery shopping? How do you use it? Did you know that you can use your smartphone to save money? In the past, we used to cut out coupons from magazines and newspapers to save money on different grocery items; now, you can save money using yo	"Did you know that you can use your smartphone to save money?" I would not use too much inflection (or pause too long after) in order to portray this as a rhetorical question.	
	ur phone! Checkout 51 is an application that I use which lists the coupons you can use to save money. If you purchase any items eligible for coupons, all you have to do is snap a picture of the		

• Supporting fact #2	receipt and the money builds up on your account. Once it reaches $20, you can request a cheque that will be sent to your home. No more cutting out coupons, no more forgetting them when you go out to shop. Save money using your smartphone.
• Supporting fact #3	
Third speaking point	The third and final way you can use your smartphone is when you sleep.
• Supporting fact #1	Sleep is quite a problem for those of us that lead busy lives. We can't seem to get enough of it and we can't seem to get quality sleep either. How many of you feel like you don't get enough sleep or enough quality sleep? Did
• Supporting fact #2	

• Supporting fact #3	identify optimal times for sleep, optimal length of sleep time and other ways to get better sleep – all through using your smartphone!	voice in volume to show excitement on how you can get the most out of your smartphone.

Conclusion	I have showed you how you can use your smartphone in three different areas of your life: using Evernote to get rid of paper, using Checkout 51 to save money on groceries and using Sleep as Android to sleep better.	
		I timed myself going through my speech and clocked it under 5 minutes. I usually prepare enough material for about 5 - 6 minutes and give myself about a minute to do pauses, allow for laughter if there is any, etc. so I decided to add in some material to help make the speech more inclusive of audience members with iphones or even those without smartphones. A good thing to remember is to make sure that your topic is accessible and inclusive of the audience and if it isn't, make sure to talk about why or to address those concerns at some point in your speech, otherwise those specific audience members may disagree, or worse, stop listening to you.
	Evernote and Checkout 51 is on Android and iTunes but there's an app on the iTunes store called Sleep Cycle alarm clock which will do similar things as Sleep as Android. Just because you do not have a smartphone does not mean you cannot take advantage of these apps that I have mentioned. For those of you without smartphones, you can use Evernote and Checkout 51 on the web. There is also a web app called sleepytime that will help you decide when to wake up or when to sleep based on the average sleep cycles.	
	There are a huge number of applications out there that can help you with any problems you face - all you have to do the next time you have a problem is search for the problem that you have with 'app' and even you might say "there's an app for that".	"HUGE" - slight increase in volume and pronounced slightly slower to emphasize the size of the app market

"and even you might say (pause and smile) there's an app for that" - delivered in a 'matter of fact' tone as if you had just proven someone wrong |

Day 6 - Full practice and crafting your introduction

At this point, you should have all of the components of your speech, perhaps not all of the components of a fantastic speech (this is out of the scope for this book), but certainly the components to deliver a well-crafted speech. If you followed along in the book, you will have two different outlines: an outline of your speech with body language and an outline of your speech with vocal variety. You might be asking yourself how you are going to practice with two different 'speeches' – and I would reply in a cheeky way "one at a time".

I think the way to approach this is to practice the outline with the vocal variety first and then practice the outline with your body language. I suggest this way because when you practice your speech with vocal variety, you will start to use body language that feels natural to you. In order to incorporate more body language into your speech, you will only have to notice where it does not feel as natural, and practice using your body language to emphasize a certain point in your speech until it does feel natural (or at least, not as uncomfortable as when you first tried to incorporate body language). Also, it is easier to practice your vocal variety (even if you do so silently in your head) than it is to practice body language. If you are like me, you will need to be in a comfortable place to practice body language while speaking but you can practice vocal variety on the bus, if you wanted to, in your head or while daydreaming.

If you have not quite memorized your speech, refer back to the memorization technique on Day 3 and take some time to memorize your speech. If you find that you do not have enough time to memorize your speech AND practice your body language or vocal variety, my suggestion would be to focus your time on memorizing your speech so that you can maintain eye contact with the audience as much as possible. The body language and vocal variety can come later; you will also have natural body language and vocal variety in your speech even if you are not an experienced public speaker. As I mentioned previously, I am an advocate for body language and vocal variety that seems natural and not forced. If you do not have the time to practice body language or vocal variety until it seems natural, my opinion is it would be better to leave it out rather than risk using a technique that confuses your audience (due to your body saying one thing and your mouth saying another).

As you practice your speech (in a mirror or recording yourself on your webcam or phone would be good), watch for a few things that might take away from your speech and try to reduce or eliminate them as much as possible:

Speech don't checklist	
Question	Action
Do you notice yourself saying a lot of crutch words? (Ah, um, so, but, and, etc.) Do you notice yourself trying to fill in empty space when you are trying to think of the next thing to say?	Be aware of the silence and embrace it – silence is a part of any speech. My strategy for getting rid of crutch words is to get rid of them completely, not just in your speech but also in your everyday speaking. If you are in a pinch however, practice a sentence in your speech, pausing and then continuing to the next sentence without any crutch words. (Feel free to use paper for this). Once you have memorized your speech, practice this from memory. A common mistake that I myself make is to get ahead of myself (I am so worried thinking about what I will say that I forget what I am currently talking about).
Does your head move around quite often? Do you blink a lot? Do you smack your lips?	Try focusing on three particular audience members so that your head does not move erratically (the three audience members should be on the left, centre and right sides of the room so that it looks as if you are looking at everyone in the audience). Blinking is not as much of a 'crutch' but it can give the audience the sense that you are nervous (and this might pose the question of why you are so nervous). Make sure you hydrate and get enough practice so that you are confident in your material. The lip smacking is difficult to eliminate; it is something that you will have to consciously practice not doing so I would not bother if there are other speech don'ts that you can focus your time on instead.

Speech don'ts checklist	
Question	**Action**
Do you find yourself leaning on one leg or the other? Do you cross your legs as you stand? Do you find your shoulders slumped down?	Remember the power pose? Try it the next time before you do a speech to gain confidence in yourself. Try to stand up straight and have your shoulders pushed slightly back and your legs shoulder width apart. Not only does this project confidence (think of a soldier saluting his officer) but it also helps give your lungs the full room to expand which helps give you more 'air' to speak with. This is another reason why you rarely see speakers sitting down as they speak unless they have to.
Do you find your hands clasped in front of you or crossed in front of you? Are you gripping your notes in front of you?	Sometimes when we get up to speak and we are nervous, we project our nervous energy into something we do physically. When we clasp our hands or closely grip our notes, it not only shows that we are nervous but it also limits the hand gestures that we can do (either naturally or practiced). If you do not clasp your hands but are speaking behind a podium or lectern, you may have a tendency to grip the podium or lectern as you are talking. Again, this is something to watch out for and to be conscious of because gripping the podium or lectern means your hand gestures will be limited.
Do you find yourself stumbling around on words a lot as you speak?	Note the areas in your speech where there is a long word to pronounce or complex phrases that you need to get the wording just right. Practice these areas until its second nature AND when you actually deliver these lines, slow down your natural rate of speaking just a little bit to make sure that you are not saying things too quickly. Better to say things right the first time than to repeat yourself or stumble upon it multiple times.

Speech don'ts checklist	
Question	**Action**
Do you say "thank you" at the end of your speech?	As you are the one speaking, the audience should be thanking you and not the other way around. It might be appropriate during times you have nothing else to say at the end of your speech (and I have done it a few times myself) but also think about how you were introduced onto the stage (usually by a host or MC) and after you end your speech, you are now 'giving' the stage back to them.
Do you apologize for not being more prepared or for not being a good communicator?	Don't apologize for things that the audience would not have known if you did not mention it in the first place. Does the audience know how much you prepared? Not if you don't tell them. Does the audience know that you haven't been speaking all of your life on this subject? Again, don't let the audience in on your secret; deliver a good speech and they will be none the wiser. As you have probably heard before, fake it till you make it.

I encourage you to be aware of the nervous tics that you have as you are delivering your speech. Better yet, enlist the help of friends to help you be aware of what nervous tics you have as it can be difficult to be self-aware of your abilities as you are giving your speech.

Crafting your introduction

Much of this content is from the "Top 10 ways to make your speech more impactful" but I will add in a few more things that I have learned since then.

The speaker's introduction is a way to bridge the gap between the speaker and the audience. If your goal as a speaker is to reach every single person in the audience, then I think it is good to assume that your audience knows nothing about you, nothing about your experience or expertise on the subject and especially nothing about what you will be talking about. A great introduction answers three questions:

1.   What is your name and speech title?

Who will the audience congratulate and thank after you deliver your speech? All joking aside, your name is a very obvious thing to provide so that you can receive recognition and credit for your speech as well as to build your own personal brand. Providing your name will also help to make your speech more personable (our speaker will be speaking on Android phones, give him a warm welcome vs. our speaker will be speaking on Android phones, give Wang a warm welcome). You will see in the next tip why providing your speech title can be a great way of making your speech more impactful.

2.   What is your experience or expertise on the subject? What makes you qualified to talk about this subject?

If a lawyer came in to talk about the latest cancer treatments, what would you think about the content of his speech? Even if the content was all true, it would be hard to believe that a lawyer would know so much about medicine.

Whoever asked you to do the speech believes that you are the right person, even if you don't believe in it yourself (although you should!). Provide as much background as you can on your expertise or experience on the speech subject. If the subject is on cancer treatments, ask yourself what evidence you can provide that can help give the audience the confidence to believe in your message and the content of your speech. Are you a doctor? Are you an oncologist? How many patients have you treated successfully? Are you the foremost researcher on cancer? A particular type of cancer? Have you written papers? All of the answers to these questions will help provide your introduction and build your credibility!

3.   Why is this subject relevant to the audience? More specifically, why is THIS subject relevant to THIS audience?

The first two questions introduce you, your speech title and why you might be a credible speaker, but if the audience does not understand why you are talking to them about this subject, your message will not get through to them. If an oncologist who is the foremost expert on cancer treatments, talks to an audience of pilots, what will the audience take away from the oncologist? It is a good idea to address this through the speech introduction so that the audience can at least start to understand why you are speaking. One problem speakers make is that because they have too much knowledge and wisdom to share, they go over the time limit. Explaining why this speech might be valuable to the audience may be a part of your speech, but that can be done with the speech introduction (or enhanced with the introduction).

Crafting your introduction template

What is your name?	
What is the title of your speech?	
What is the purpose of your speech?	
What is your expertise or experience on the subject? What makes you qualified to speak on this subject?	
Why is this subject relevant to your audience? What do you hope that they can take away after listening to you speak?	

Once you have answered these questions, you can then start to craft the whole introduction. Do not worry if you only have one sentence for each question, keeping your introduction short and concise can be a very good thing as well (are audiences there to listen to your introduction or to listen to you as a speaker?).

Example introduction for "There's an app for that"

Here is an example template filled out to help guide my introduction for my speech:

What is your name?	Wang Yip
What is the title of your speech?	"There's an app for that"
What is the purpose of your speech?	To introduce people to the idea of 'apps' and that they can get a lot more value out of their smartphone that they aren't already getting.
What is your expertise or experience on the subject? What makes you qualified to speak on this subject?	I am a huge Android fan, keeping up with the latest games and apps and trying out anything that I find interesting. I work in IT consulting and before that I worked as an Emerging Technologies Specialist and in both jobs, I regularly read up on the latest technology and try to understand how the technology would be useful.
Why is this subject relevant to your audience? What do you hope that they can take away after listening to you speak?	Almost everyone currently has or will have a smartphone in the near future; however, I believe that not everyone realizes the power that is in their smartphone and the value that it can provide to their lives. I hope that after the speech, the audience will learn of three new apps that can improve their lives and appreciate that there are many problems that apps can solve.

This becomes:

> Our speaker will be sharing his knowledge on Android and applications or 'apps' for short. Apps are software that you can install on your phone to solve a specific problem. Little do people know that these apps can help improve your life in small and meaningful ways. Our speaker is a huge Android fan and he currently works as an IT consultant but has previously worked as an Emerging Technologies Specialist. In both roles, he reads up on the latest trends and technology and tries to understand how to apply it to his life to be more productive. Estimates say that about 70% of the population will have smartphones in 2017 (about 60% of the adult population) and there's a good chance that you either currently have a smartphone or will get a smartphone in the near future. If you do not have a smartphone now, this might give you a push to the other side and help give you another reason why you might switch. Today, he will be sharing his experience on how to get more value out of your smartphone with apps for Android, the iPhone and for those of you without smartphones, the web. Please give a warm welcome to Wang, with a speech entitled "There's an app for that".

Sometimes the person introducing you will ad-lib so you may want to specify to him/her that you want the introduction read word for word as much as possible. Although the person introducing you may have done speaker introductions before, it can be variable and if there is even the slightest possibility that the introduction is not done well, it may throw off your whole speech. Therefore, providing a solid introduction that you have crafted and that fits into your overall message of your speech can ensure that your introduction is done properly, and it is one less thing to worry about before you deliver your

Last saved: July 15, 15

speech.

Day 7 - Final touches and delivering your speech

It is the day of your speech, are you nervous? Don't be – you have written out your speech, polished it with your own style of vocal variety and body language and understand the different nervous tics that might prevent your speech from being the best it can be.

This last day, I want to talk about any logistics you need to be aware of during your speech, your speaking area, how to project confidence, how to relax your audience and finally some tactics on what to do when your speech is going well and when your speech is not going so well.

Last minute logistics checklist

This checklist will help to make sure that you are not missing anything just before delivering your speech. It is handy to go through this list the morning of the speech so that you can make sure that everything that is needed to support your speech is in place and that you don't have to worry about it during your speech (or worse, just before your speech starts).

Last minute checklist	
Question	**Action**
Will you have a microphone when you speak? How will all of the audience hear you?	Take note of any background noise that is in the room. Is there a fan / air conditioner in the room? Is there a buzzing noise from the fluorescent lights? Will you be talking through a meal (i.e., will people be noisily eating at the same time?)
	All of these factors should help you determine what volume you should be projecting your voice. If you have use of a microphone, make sure that you are holding the microphone close to your mouth at all times to provide consistent volume. This also means that vocal variety might not be as effective through the microphone as the microphone serves to amplify your volume – it will take a more drastic change in your voice to make vocal variety more apparent to your audience.

Last minute checklist	
Question	**Action**
Will you have a podium / lectern to speak from?	The best thing is for you to memorize your speech so that you do not need the use of the podium or lectern; however, in the case that you do need your notes, try to use cue cards instead which can be held in your hand and do not limit your hands as much as a sheet of notes do.
	Feel free to move the podium / lectern so that you are able to use the full speaking area (if it is in the middle and you have to walk around it as you speak, it should be moved).
Do you feel confident about your speech?	Even if you don't, don't worry! Make sure to smile a lot during your speech and fake it until you make it. The audience can't tell if you are faking confidence or if you actually have confidence and by smiling, you will relax the audience which will give you even more confidence to proceed with your speech. Here is a secret that not many speakers know: the audience wants you to succeed; the audience wants you to wow them; and the audience wants you to get through to them. The audience does not want you to fail; they are on your side! Deliver a great speech and wow them!

Last minute checklist	
Question	**Action**
Are you using technology?	In my experience, technology seems to always fail when you need it to work. Arrive at the venue early and test your laptop. Make sure that you bring a power cord and that you have all the right connector cables and backups of the slides / images / whatever you want to show (either through the cloud, a USB stick or on a separate folder somewhere).
	Test, test and test again. Do not ever try to do a speech without testing any technology you are using beforehand because if it does fail (and there's a possibility it will), it will disrupt your speech and you as a speaker.
	If you insist on using technology, make sure to have a backup plan of some sort. This can include:
	• A print out of the slides for all audience members
	• A flip chart that shows all relevant facts (must be legible by all audience members)
Are you using props?	Make sure that your props are visible to the whole audience. If it is something small, make sure that you use descriptive language to describe it (as if you were describing something that the audience could not see) so that anybody that cannot see it is not left out. Props that can be seen by the whole audience will have a better impact than props that cannot be seen.
Are you using anything visual that the audience has to read?	Again, like props, anything that the audience has to read should be in ridiculously large font (the bigger, the better). It also serves to make sure that your message is as concise as possible (you certainly do not want your audience to be reading an essay off of your flip chart or a paragraph off of your PowerPoint presentation).

This checklist is quite short as when things are going well, there aren't too many things to keep in mind. Your confidence will be brimming, you will have the right pauses, your body language will feel natural, your vocal variety will 'wow' the audience and the audience will be both receptive and attentive to what you have to say.

The 'dandy' checklist	
Question	**Action**
Are you smiling a lot throughout your speech?	It shows you're having fun, you're brimming with confidence and you are enjoying yourself. Smiling is a great way to relax the audience and to project enormous amounts of confidence in yourself and your speech.
Are you pausing in all the right places?	Pausing will seem like an afterthought; you will pause in all the right places and the speech will seem really 'quick' to you but everything will fall in place and before you know it, you will be done.
Is the pace of your speech not too fast and not too slow?	You will speed up during times when you are excited or feeling passionate about your speech and you will slow down when you really want to emphasize a particular part of your speech. The audience won't be struggling to
Is your body language effective?	You aren't slouching and you have a 'presence' in front of the audience. Your body language is purposeful and you do not have any nervous tics or fidgeting that would otherwise show that you aren't sure about something as you speak.
Is the audience reacting positively to your speech?	As you say certain points, look to specific people in the audience. Some people will unconsciously give you feedback as you deliver your speech (e.g., they will nod their heads in agreement or they may mutter their agreement). This feedback can be used to adjust your speech as necessary (e.g., if you see confused looks, you may wish to slow down your speech or re-explain something that you have just said that might have been confusing).

Last saved: July 15, 15

When your speech is not going well

When your speech is not going well, there are many things you can do to get back on track. I have provided a number of different situations and tactics that you can use to when you encounter issues during your speech.

The 'mayday' checklist		
	Situation	**Tactic**
	You have a lot of um's and ah's during your speech.	Try to slow down the pace of your speech and concentrate on not using crutch words to fill in the silence when you are not speaking. In the grand scheme of things, having crutch words is not as important as getting your message across.
	You are fidgeting a lot during your speech.	Try to concentrate on the words of your speech. Try not to have anything in your hands that you can fidget with (e.g., clickable pens, paper, etc.).
	You are pacing back and forth and find yourself moving around a lot as you are speaking.	If you find yourself moving around a lot, stick to a specific spot on the ground and keep yourself there. Do not try to move around too much otherwise it will be very distracting for the audience and all they can concentrate on will be your movement rather than your speech.

The 'mayday' checklist	
Situation	**Tactic**
You have suddenly lost your place in your speech and you have no idea what next to talk about.	There are actually several tactics you can use to help you with your speech: • If you have your notes handy, tell the audience "This next part is extremely important and I want to get the wording just right" and then take a glance through your notes to make sure you do not lose your place again. • If you do not have your notes handy, try to go over your speech again from the very beginning by summarizing what you have talked about so far. Sometimes when you talk about what you have talked about, it will jog your memory on what to say next, especially if your speech is laid out in a logical manner. • Make it up! If all else fails, try to make something up. This tactic works only if your speech has that kind of flexibility but it can do wonders and
You have completely lost the audience on something you just explained.	First, it takes awareness of the audience's reaction to your speech in order to understand when you lost them. Once you see that the audience is losing their way in your speech, backtrack a little bit and ask the audience if they need something to be explained again. If you still see confused looks, backtrack some more and start explaining things from the very beginning. It also helps to have an analogy or example that your audience can use to hook on to.
You realize that you suddenly have lost all use of your technology (e.g., your laptop has died, the projector has failed, etc.)	Do not panic – you have already prepared for this situation by having a backup plan. The last time this happened to me, I was not ready for it and my speech ended up going over as I was carefully explaining every slide. Have printouts ready for your audience or have a backup plan that you know will not fail (flipcharts rarely fail to work).

The 'mayday' checklist	
Situation	**Tactic**
You find yourself stumbling over words even though you never had any problems when you were practicing your speech.	Try to slow down the pace of your speech. When you get nervous (and even the most seasoned speakers get nervous sometimes before a big speech), the rate of your speaking goes up. This, in combination with your mouth becoming very dry may cause you to trip on certain words. If you know that a big word is coming up, do not be afraid to pause and slowly e-nun-ci-ate before continuing on at a regular pace.
You find yourself running out of time.	Depending on your venue and the reason for your speech, this might be something to worry about or this might be something to just note for the future. If it is important to end on time, start to ruthlessly cut down on your content until you have just enough to get through your material and then conclude promptly. Unfortunately, you may lose the message of your speech but you will have to make compromises in order to end the speech on time. If it is not important, do be mindful of the audience's time and try not to take up too much of their time. At some point, the audience will look at their watches and if they see you are terribly over time, the only thing on their mind is why your speech wasn't as concise as it could have been.
You realize as you go through your speech that you have forgotten a few things.	Don't worry, it happens! If it does not disrupt your overall speech then make sure to include it (for instance, if you were supposed to mention how this specific point relates to the overall problem, mention it for the next point OR wait until the conclusion to talk about how all the points relate back to the overall problem). If it will disrupt your overall speech (i.e., the flow of the speech) then just leave it out. As speakers, we only have so much time to deliver a message and the audience knows that we cannot possibly fit everything in so leave it for another speech or for a Q & A session after.

These tactics should help with some of the more common situations that speakers get into when their speech isn't going well for them. *Knock on wood*, hopefully you will never encounter these particular situations but if you do, at least you will have a few tactics to help you get through the situations. The best way to prevent the situation from happening is practice and to have a backup plan just in case.

After the speech

Congratulations! You have completed your speech and have taken a step towards gaining more confidence in public speaking. If you have a good friend in the audience (and I mean a really good friend), ask him/her what things went well and what things didn't go well. Silently be thankful that you have such a good friend and note down the things that they said so that you can improve upon them for the next time you speak.

Jot down a few notes about your own speech and how you felt – or get a friend/acquaintance in the audience to judge how you delivered your speech using the following simple checklist. If you don't know anyone in the audience or don't want to make a new friend, just fill out the checklist with how you felt the speech went. Self-reflection can be a great way to learn about what works and what doesn't work for next time. I know how it feels to be your own harshest critic but don't be too hard on yourself – you accomplished something awesome after all!

Instructions for the evaluator: Judge the speaker on how they delivered the speech rather than the content of their speech. As you are listening to the speech, jot down notes on specific times in the speech that you noticed something strange. With most evaluations of speeches, you will be judging from what you think is best; the speaker will love you for the feedback and incorporate what he/she thinks is best.

Evaluating the speaker checklist	
Question	**Comments**
Did the speaker seem comfortable and confident during the speech?	
Do you feel like the audience was receptive to the speech? Did they laugh? Did they nod their heads? Etc.	
How was the vocal variety? Was the speech monotonous or did the speaker have a variety of tones in their speech to keep things interesting?	

Evaluating the speaker checklist	
How was the body language of the speaker? Did they seem nervous or did they seem confident? Did they have any nervous tics?	
How did the speech flow? Was it logical from one point to the next?	
Was the speech easy to follow? Was it organized in a way that helped the audience to understand the purpose of the speech?	
Did the speaker's introduction pique your interest? Did it give you enough background or context to help you understand the speech?	
Did the speaker have any lapse in memory during the speech?	
Did you hear the speaker say any crutch words? Where in the speech did you hear them? What specific crutch words did they use? Did they primarily use crutch words at the start of sentences? End of sentences?	

Evaluating the speaker checklist	
Could you hear the speaker? Was the volume loud enough for everyone in the audience to hear?	
Did the speaker use props or visual aids? Were they legible and easy to see / read?	
Did the speaker use a PowerPoint presentation? Did they just read off the slides?	
Did the speaker have good eye contact with the audience or did they look down or up frequently?	
Did the speaker go over their time limit? Did the speaker have to rush to get through their speech?	

Bonus video and evaluation!

As a special bonus, I am sending you a link to me delivering the very speech that I created in this e-book. I will use as much body language, vocal variety, etc., as I can to deliver the speech and you can see this in all of its glory in the video. I will also take some time to critique my own speech and to point out areas of improvement. As some people say, there is no such thing as a perfect speech and I do not claim to be close to delivering perfect speeches (though I'd like to think that I have come close). In this way, I hope this will help solidify the examples that I have talked about in this e-book and help give you some ideas on how to craft and deliver your own speech.

Here it is: http://www.youtube.com/watch?v=ft7XdlBFWp8&t=1m6s

It starts at 1 minute 6 seconds as I did the speech in a Toastmaster setting. I have speech objectives that I was working from and I had a fairly long introduction (or at least it felt long to me). If you want to listen to my objectives, please feel free to listen from the start but I have fast forwarded the link to my introduction and then subsequent speech.

Self-critique:

- My biggest issue with my speech was that I went over time. The speech was supposed to be a 5 – 7 minute speech and I ended up going over by about a minute and a half. Luckily for me, I was in a safe environment at Toastmasters (one of the many good things about being part of Toastmasters) but you certainly do not want to go over time as a keynote speaker at a conference or as part of a workshop for clients because the audience will feel that you do not respect their time (or that you think that your time is more valuable than theirs).

- If I were to do my speech the next time, I think I would have spent less time on the first app.

- As I finished talking about the first app and started talking about the second app, I realized that I had missed a few key points in my speech that I wanted to discuss (i.e., how the app is not just on the Android platform but also on iOS and on the web so that anybody, even those without a smartphone, can use it). I decided to forego all this and discuss it at the end.

- As you probably can tell between the script and the video, I did not follow the script word for word. I decided to memorize key points and change up the speech so that instead of getting into the material in a roundabout way, I jumped straight in and got to the three areas that I was going to focus on. I thought this would be more effective than what I originally had.

- I asked quite a few questions and I felt that this was a good way of engaging the audience. When used sporadically throughout the speech, this can be a very good way of engaging the audience but if you use it too much then the speech turns into a workshop or discussion.

Feedback received from the audience / my evaluator:

- The evaluator liked lots of things about my speech:
  - Organization
  - Applicability of the apps to the audience (these were all things that anybody could relate to)

Last saved: July 15, 15

- o   Purposeful body language and movement
- o   Confidence
- Great voice and volume
- Very well organized
- Easy to follow
- Great ending
- You made it look easy
- You had a warm style
- You seemed very engaged in your topic and you seemed sincerely friendly in your approach
- Very relevant information
- Well prepared
- Instead of "I'm going to explain a situation" open with "I have a mountain of paper" – maybe bring a pile in
- You related well to the audience
- I would have liked to see more props, see the app working (at least screen shots)
- Overall well done, well organized and very enjoyable

Thank You

Before you go and create a speech (haha no seriously just go do it), I'd like to express my gratitude for purchasing my e-book. I know you could have picked from dozens of books about public speaking, but you took a chance with me and I greatly appreciate it.

Now I'd like to ask for a small favour. <u>Could you please take a minute or two and leave a review for this book on Amazon?</u>

This feedback will help me continue to write great Kindle books that help you get the results you are looking for.

More Kindle eBooks by Wang

<u>Make your speech more impactful</u> – 10 tips (+ 1 bonus tip) on delivering an impactful speech.

<u>100+ Tips For Speakers</u> – 100+ tips for speakers on a range of topics including preparing for a speech, delivering a speech and concluding a speech (and everything in between)

<u>A Guide to Evaluating Speeches</u> – How to prepare, construct and provide impactful evaluations

www.ingramcontent.com/pod-product-compliance
Lightning Source LLC
Chambersburg PA
CBHW060339290526
45793CB00003B/670